ROAD TRIP

by Michael Sandler
illustrated by Nicole Wong

Harcourt
SCHOOL PUBLISHERS

May 25

I am so excited! Dad says that we are driving across the whole country this summer. We will rent a van. The trip will be a month long! We will visit relatives in Missouri and California. We will see the sights along the way. We will camp in many different places.

I have never been outside of Florida. This trip is going to be fun. It's only a month away.

May 28

I talked to Mr. Hale, my science teacher, about our trip today. He took out a map of the United States. We found all the places I will be traveling through. We talked about the different kinds of landscapes. I'll see mountains, prairies, forests, and deserts. He wants me to take notes. Then I can give a report to the class about the trip when I come back to school in the fall.

June 22

Finally, we are on our way. Today we left on our trip to the West. The first part was kind of boring. I had driven past these places before. It was more interesting once we got out of Florida.

We stopped for the night in Memphis, Tennessee. Dad took us to a barbecue restaurant that is supposed to be the best in the country. The food was delicious. Tomorrow we'll go to Kansas City, Missouri. We will spend a few days with my cousins.

5

June 27

Staying with my cousins in Kansas City was fun, but I was anxious to continue with the trip. Finally, we were on our way again.

The scenery in Kansas doesn't change much as you drive through it. We drove mile after mile through flat, flat land. There are no mountains. I didn't even notice any hills. However, the land wasn't bare. There was field after field of corn and wheat. Some of these fields seemed to stretch on for miles. The plants waved in the breeze. The land looked like a green and gold ocean!

Kansas is part of the Great Plains. Mr. Hale had told me about this area before we left. The Great Plains is a huge area of prairie. Prairie is land without many trees. A lot of the Great Plains is farmland. Other parts are too hot and dry for crops to grow.

July 2

Wow! That is all I can say. The Rocky Mountains are incredible. The road began to rise after we left Kansas and entered Colorado. The prairie became less flat. In places, there were hills.

After a few hours, I saw the mountains rising up in front of us. I knew mountains were bigger than hills. I had never seen mountains except in pictures. The Rockies looked like a great wall of rock reaching up into the sky. Seeing these famous mountains for myself was very exciting.

We spent three days camping in the Rockies. One thing that surprised me was the change in temperature. The air got much cooler as we went higher into the mountains. I had to wear a sweater even though it was the middle of the summer.

It was freezing in our tent last night, but my sleeping bag kept me warm. The weather didn't feel like July. It felt more like December. Some of the mountains here still have snow on them.

9

July 6

I don't need that sweatshirt anymore! It's not cold outside, and there is no snow. In fact, there is hardly water of any kind. We've left the high mountains behind. Now we're in the desert in Utah.

We studied deserts in Mr. Hale's class. Deserts are places where it hardly rains. They get less water than prairies do. Some deserts are so dry that they have almost no animal or plant life. Mr. Hale told us that rain does not fall for years in some deserts!

This desert is called the Great Basin Desert. It's not as dry as some deserts. There are bushes and grass. Animals live here. Today I saw lizards and squirrels when we stopped in a park for lunch.

10.

July 8

Deserts are fun, but I don't think I would like to live in one. Now we are in a desert in the state of Nevada. It's just too dry. You don't see any cornfields here. There's not enough water. I think I would turn into a lizard if I lived here.

I'm feeling a little homesick. Maybe it's the ocean. I'm always near the water at home in Florida. I miss it. Luckily, we are getting closer to the Pacific Ocean. However, we need to cross another set of mountains before we reach it. They are called the Sierra Nevada.

11

July 11

Wow, this is the best part so far. We're camping in a forest in the Sierra Nevada. The forest is just amazing. It is filled with the biggest trees I've ever seen. The trees are called giant sequoias. I am taking lots of pictures for my report. The kids in class won't believe the size of these trees.

A park ranger told us about the giant sequoia trees. He says the giant sequoias grow for hundreds of years. They can live for three thousand years!

Some are almost 300 feet (91m) tall. They are also very big around. If you laid one down along a road, it could block three lanes of traffic.

July 15

Water is everywhere! We've reached the ocean again! Last night we arrived at Grandma Clara's house. She lives in Monterey, California. Today she took us to the beach. The sea is beautiful. It's a darker blue than it is in Florida.

It's also much colder. Still, it felt so good to jump into the water. Grandma wants to know everything about the trip. She wants to know what we did. She wants us to tell her everything we saw. Tomorrow my photos will be ready. She'll be able to see for herself.

13

July 22

I can't believe the trip is almost over. This morning we said good-bye to Grandma. Then we drove to the airport. We dropped off our rental minivan. We'll be home in Miami in a few hours.

It was quite a trip. We drove over 3,000 miles (4,800 km). We saw all kinds of landscapes—prairie, desert, forests, and mountains. As soon as I get home, I'll start working on my report. Mr. Hale told me to try to write one page. That's going to be tough, though. I think I might have to write ten!

14

Scaffolded Language Development

USING COMPARATIVES Tell students that comparatives are adjectives used to compare two things. Some comparatives are formed with the word *more* and an adjective, such as *more difficult*. Others are formed by adding -er to the adjective, such as *funnier.* Review the following sentences from the story with students. Point out the comparative in each sentence.

It was more interesting *once we got out of Florida.* (page 5)
I knew mountains were bigger *than hills.* (page 8)

Then have students find other comparatives in the story.

It's a darker blue than it is in Florida. (page 13)
It's also much colder. (page 13)

 Science

Scenery Sketch Review the different types of landscapes described in this story. Then help students make a chart to compare the landscapes.

School-Home Connection

Talk About Trips Ask students to have family members describe trips they have taken. Have them name favorite places they visited and explain what they liked about them.

Word Count: 1,094